Educational Skits Combined Set #1

Jill Hierstein-Morris

Published by CREATIVELY YOURS PUBLICATIONS, 2024.

Table of Contents

Book 1
BEHAVIORS

A HORSE OF A DIFFERENT COLOR
TEASING

CAST: Bernie, a blue horse—-Bunny

Approximately 5 Minutes

by Jill Hierstein-Morris

© 2024 Creatively Yours Publications

(Blue horse enters humming. Bunny enters hopping.)

BUNNY: Wow! Look at you! I must say, you're a horse of a different color. How silly you look. A blue horse. (Laughs).

BERNIE: (Shyly). I was born a blue horse.

BUNNY: (Sarcastically). Oh, really? I thought you fell into a can of paint. Blue horse, blue horse, silly looking blue horse. What's your name? Blue Boy?

BERNIE: My name is Bernie.

BUNNY: Bernie Blue, Bernie Blue, what a silly horse are you. (Looks around). I'm going to tell my friends about you Bernie Blue, so they can have a good laugh too. (Bunny exits.)

BERNIE: (Talking to audience). That bunny was very rude! His teasing could make me blue, I mean sad, except for one thing. I know that by teasing me he is only trying to get attention or make himself feel more important. I suppose it would amuse him to make me angry. That's why I didn't fight back.

(Bernie asks questions. Give the audience a chance to respond after each one.)

Has anyone ever teased YOU because they think you are too short?

Or too tall?

Too big? Or too small?

Because your hair curls, or it won't?

Because you like things that they don't?

Because you have a big nose?

Or wear different clothes?

Because you're a different color?

Or somehow differ from another?

Well, consider this: There are billions of people and animals in this world, and no two are exactly alike. That's right. Even twins have something unique about them. And there is NOTHING wrong with being different. That's what makes you, you. Every one of our differences can be something a not-so-nice person could tease us about. But differences can also be things a nice person might praise us for.

Wouldn't you be happier if everyone found something nice to say about you? It could be your smile, your clothes, your talents in art, music, dance or sports. It could be all kinds of things. Everyone has far more good qualities than bad ones. I believe in treating others as you would like to be treated. Would you rather be teased or praised? (Pause for response). Me, too! (He looks and sees Bunny approaching.) Oh, oh, here comes that bunny again. (Bunny enters hopping and chanting). Blue horse. Blue horse. Silly Bernie blue horse.

BERNIE: Hi, Bunny. I just noticed what beautiful eyes you have.

BUNNY: Huh? Oh, thank you.

BERNIE: And what a fine white tooth. I'm sure it comes in very handy for biting through carrots.

BUNNY: Why, yes. I am very proud of it. Um, you know, Bernie, I am sorry about teasing you. You really are a very pretty shade of blue.

BERNIE: Thank you, Bunny.

BERNIE: I know where there is a field of plump juicy carrots. Should we go get some?

BUNNY: (Patting the horse's back). You bet, friend.

(They exit together.)

TEASING

[1] Write or discuss some of the things you have been teased about and how you reacted to the teasing.

[2] Set aside one full day, including both home and school, to sincerely praise everything that's good about the people around you. Write or discuss how people reacted and how it made you feel.

[3] Fold a plain sheet of paper in half. On one side draw pictures to indicate the things you have been teased about. On the other side, draw things you feel are praiseworthy about you. Are the same things on each side? Could they be? Share your drawings with friends and classmates.

[4] Find examples of teasing on television programs. Write or discuss what was said and how the object of the teasing reacted. Would you have reacted the same way? Discuss how the relationship between the people effects their reactions to teasing. (Teasing a friend may be fun, but to an acquaintance or stranger, it would be rude.)

[5] Write or discuss an imaginary world where everyone looks the same, dresses the same, likes the same things and has the same talents. What are the good things about such an imaginary world? What are the bad things? Would you prefer living in the real world or the imaginary one? Why?

IT'S A LIE – WHEN AND WHY?

LYING

CAST: 2 Boys or Girls

Approximately 5 Minutes

by Jill Hierstein-Morris

© 2024 Creatively Yours Publications

(Kelly enters, then Chris.)

CHRIS: Hi Kelly.

KELLY: Hi. Where have you been? You're late.

CHRIS: I was ready to walk out the door when Tommy's phone rang. He told me he didn't want to talk, and to answer and say he wasn't there.

KELLY: Did you?

CHRIS: Sure.

KELLY: But if he was there, you told a lie.

CHRIS: I told him it was a lie. But he said it was okay because it was just a "little white lie."

KELLY: Lies don't have colors. A lie is a lie.

CHRIS: Oh, c'mon Kelly. I've heard you lie before.

KELLY: No, you haven't!

CHRIS: Yes, I have. You told me you saw a green hairy monster coming out of a flying saucer in the park.

KELLY: Oh, that's not a lie. I just said that for fun. I knew it wasn't true...And you knew it wasn't true. We were pretending. That's not a lie. It's a fantasy, make-believe statement.

CHRIS: What about the time you fell and said your leg was broken? It wasn't.

KELLY: I thought it was. I couldn't walk on it. And it really hurt! The doctors said it was just a bad sprain. But I didn't lie. It was just a mistake. Everyone makes mistakes.

CHRIS: Well, remember the day you didn't study for the big math test in Miss Harrison's class? You told your mother you were sick so you wouldn't have to go to school.

KELLY: Yes. I did lie then. I wasn't sick. I didn't want to take the test.

CHRIS: So, see, you do lie.

KELLY: I USED to. But I don't any more. Mom stopped believing me when I said I was sick. Last week she made me go to school when I really did feel awful.

CHRIS: Yes That's the problem with lies. People stop trusting you. Or when they find out you lied to them; you are in even more trouble. It's like when I ate the cupcakes.

KELLY: What cupcakes?

CHRIS: The ones mom was saving for dad's lunches. I ate all twelve of them. When mom asked me if I ate them, I just shrugged my shoulders and got out of the kitchen, fast.

KELLY: If you knew what happened to the cupcakes, and didn't tell, you lied.

CHRIS: I told myself; I really didn't TELL a lie because I didn't say anything.

KELLY: But you led her to believe something that wasn't true. That's a lie.

CHRIS: I know. That's what mom said when she found the cupcake papers in my bedroom. When she asked how they got there, I was going to blame my brother, Tommy. But I knew she would find out the truth.

KELLY: If you lie to cover up your first lie, you're in even MORE trouble.

CHRIS: That's what I decided, so I admitted I had eaten them. I felt a lot better after I told the truth. Not so scared.

KELLY: Did your mom punish you?

CHRIS: No. I offered to buy more cupcakes with my allowance money. Mom suggested we bake more cupcakes together to replace the ones I had eaten, so we did. I missed my favorite TV program though. I have tried not to take things or to lie since that day.

KELLY: I try not to lie too. Sometimes it's very difficult. There are times people ask you if you like something, and you don't. Do you lie to make them feel good or hurt their feelings by telling truth?

CHRIS: That's a tough one. Honesty is no excuse for being rude. I can't tell my sister, "That red dress makes you look fat," without making her upset. But I could say, "The red dress is okay, but the blue one makes you look much slimmer."

KELLY: Yes. That sounds good!

CHRIS: And it wouldn't hurt her feelings.

KELLY: And it's not a lie.

CHRIS: I could feel good about telling the truth that way.

KELLY: Me, too. Everything is easier and everyone is happier when we don't tell lies.

CHRIS: Right. And the next time, Tommy will have to leave the house or answer his own phone calls.

(They exit giggling.)

LYING

[1] Fantasy is imaginative fiction with strange settings and unusual characters. Write a fantasy about an elf, pixie, giant, witch, or creature from outer space. Be specific about where they came from, their appearance, abilities, and character traits.

[2] Write specific examples of mistakes and lies you see on television programs. How are problems created and resolved? What complications are caused by lying to cover up a lie? Are the TV examples something that could happen to you? How would you handle them if they did?

[3] You have a magic camera. It takes pictures of feelings. Draw a picture of what the camera sees when you tell a lie, or when someone tells a lie to you. (Depict anger, disappointment, suspicion, or other emotion.) Write a slogan or poem to tell about the emotion in the picture.

[4] Honesty is no excuse for being rude. Discuss or demonstrate ways of telling the truth without hurting someone's feelings.

[5} George Washington, our first U.S. President, was known for his honesty. Write about another person (past or present) who is admired for his or her honesty.

RUDY GETS A RESPONSE
RUDENESS

CAST: Monster—-Two Boys – Tom & John—-Two Girls – Jane & Sue

PROP: Ball

Approximately 5 Minutes

by Jill Hierstein-Morris

© 2024 Creatively Yours Publications

(Monster runs on stage.)

MONSTER: *(to audience).* Hi! I'm so excited to be here…You see, I don't get invited to many places. *(Pause).* I'm not sure why. Some people say it's because I'm rude. Other people won't even talk to me. These days I live an uncomplicated life. I go to the park each morning and swing for hours. Sometimes other kids stand around and wait for me to get off the swings, but I don't. I like to swing.

(Monster paces.) This morning a little girl insisted it was her turn to swing and started crying. Can you imagine that? I wonder what made her think she should have a turn. I don't believe in taking turns. Do you?

JANE: *(Enters yelling).* Ice Cream. Ice Cream.

(The Monster runs up pushes the girl aside and runs off stage. Jane stands with a disgusted look on her face and hands on her hips. Then the Monster returns.)

MONSTER: Burp!

JANE: That's disgusting.

MONSTER: No, it isn't. It's funny.

JANE: It's NOT funny. It's disgusting. Excuse yourself.

MONSTER: I never say, "Excuse me," ever.

JANE: You are very rude.

MONSTER: Well, I think you are very...Fat! *(Jane exits. The monster looks around the stage, then yells.)* Hey! That's MY ball.

(Monster runs off stage and enters holding the ball. Tom follows him onto the stage.)

MONSTER: *(To boy)*. If you want to play with my ball, you will have to play with me.

TOM: Okay.

(Monster runs back and forth bouncing the ball.)

TOM: When do I get a turn?

MONSTER: When I say so. It's my ball.

TOM: You're not playing by the rules.

MONSTER: Yes I am. MY RULES.

TOM: Forget it. I don't want to play with your ball, or you. *(Exits slowly.)*

MONSTER: Hey, wait...I'm not finished playing yet. You can't leave....Oh, well.

(John and Sue enter to one side of the stage and stop to talk.)

MONSTER: Hi, John. *(John ignores him.)* John, I said hi.

SUE: *(To John).* Who is that?

JOHN: I don't know his real name. Everyone calls him Rudy because he is so rude. He's always trying to be the center of attention and interrupting when other people are talking. Just try to ignore him.

SUE: That's easier said than done.

MONSTER: Who is that girl you're with? *(No answer).* Well, whoever she is, she looks like a toad.

SUE: John, he called me a toad. *(Sobs lightly).*

JOHN: He's just trying to upset you because I wouldn't talk to him. Let's get out of here.

(They exit quickly.)

MONSTER: *(To audience).* Well, how do you like that? Who needs them? I don't need anyone. I'm glad I don't have a bunch of friends. Friends are SO demanding. They are always bothering you to play with them, they call you on the phone to chat, and they are always wanting you to go places with them. Who has time for all that nonsense?

(Pacing). I never have to worry about getting dressed up to go to parties because no one ever invites me. I used to go places with people, but I hated it. They expected me to say please and thank you all the time. They wouldn't always let me have the biggest treats or the best toys to play with. So now I play alone and do exactly what I want. Isn't that great? *(Monster waits for audience responses to the questions.)*

Do you mean you like having friends to bug you?

Do you like taking turns...and sharing?

And you don't mind having to say please and thank you?

That's amazing! Oh, well, I am excited anyway. This is the most people who have talked to me in years. You ACTUALLY talked to me. Do you think if I try to be nicer, you will want talk to me again?

(Monster *thinks for a minute.*) Then, I will try. Th...th..ank you. Thank you. Thank you.

(He smiles and skips off stage.)

FOLLOW-UP EXERCISES

RUDENESS

[1] Make a poster using "Politeness is Important" or "Courtesy is Contagious" as the theme.

[2] Discuss what self-concepts are and how rudeness or politeness effects them.

[3] Discuss rudeness in relation to exaggeration, comic effect, quest for attention and revenge. Cite examples from television, movies or books.

[4] '"Sticks and stones may break my bones, but words will never hurt me" is a common phrase. Write or discuss if this is a true statement. Why or why not?

[5] Write or discuss what techniques can be used to:

Change a rude person's attitude.

Control the negative feelings rudeness imposes on you.

Become more aware of how our words and actions affect others.

A TATTLING TALE
TATTLING

CAST: Shaggy, mother dog—-Spot, puppy

Approximately 4.5 Minutes

by Jill Hierstein-Morris

© 2024 Creatively Yours Publications

(Shaggy enters and Spot enters running.)

SPOT: Mom! Mom! Rover pushed me over and hurt my paw.

SHAGGY: I am sorry to hear that.

SPOT: And Fido called me horrible names. Fifi wouldn't show me her picture, and Max wouldn't let me in line at the drinking fountain.

SHAGGY: It sounds like you have had a rough day.

SPOT: Yes. And do you want to know what else happened?

SHAGGY: No.

SPOT: No?

SHAGGY: That's right. No. If you want my attention, you are going about it all wrong. I don't want you to be a tattletale.

SPOT: What does my tail have to do with it?

SHAGGY: Silly pup. A tattletale is someone who is ALWAYS telling on others.

SPOT: There's nothing wrong with just telling someone something is there?

SHAGGY: Let me think how to explain this...I guess it depends on WHY you are telling. There's nothing wrong with tattling if it's for safety reasons.

SPOT: What's tattling for safety reasons mean?

SHAGGY: It means, it's okay to tell someone if a person is playing with matches. That could start a fire. Or if you see someone committing a crime. Also, if someone is trying to get you to do something you know you shouldn't. It's fine to tell things that affect your safety or the safety of others.

SPOT: Like if my little sister gets into the cleanser cabinet?

SHAGGY: That's right. But YOUR tattling wouldn't be tattling for safety, would it?

SPOT: No.

SHAGGY: Then there's tattling to protect property. That would be telling when someone is writing on walls, exploring things they are too young to operate, such as the dash board of a car or playing ball where they could break windows. That wasn't the reason you were tattling, was it?

SPOT: No. What other kinds of tattling are there?

SHAGGY: There's tattling nice.

SPOT: Tattling nice?

SHAGGY: It's telling nice things that happen around you. When you notice and praise the good things other people do. It's being complimentary. But you were doing the opposite of that kind of tattling.

SPOT: Then, what kind of tattling was I doing?

SHAGGY: I would say you were tattling trouble.

SPOT: Tattling trouble? But I didn't have any trouble tattling. I told you exactly what happened.

SHAGGY: I didn't say you had trouble tattling. I said you were tattling trouble. That means you were telling on others so they would be in trouble, or so I would think you were a better dog because you weren't acting like they were.

SPOT: And that's bad?

SHAGGY: Yes, that's bad. That kind of tattling could make your friends angry. Then they may not want to play with you. They will think of you as a troublemaker.

SPOT: Oh, no.

SHAGGY: And it will make the person you tattle to, so tired of listening to you that they might not listen when you have something really important to say.

SPOT: That reminds me of "The Boy Who Cried Wolf" story.

SHAGGY: Exactly. If you run and tattle each time you have a problem, you will never learn to solve problems by yourself. And there's the danger that by tattling, you could only look for bad things that happen around you, and not look for good things.

SPOT: Okay. I'll try never to tattle again.

SHAGGY: Remember, You can tattle for safety, to protect yourself, others or property. You can tattle nice. Praise is always welcome. Just don't tattle trouble.

SPOT: Because it will end up causing ME more trouble than anyone?

SHAGGY: Right. Smart puppy.

SPOT: Mom, can I tell you something?

SHAGGY: Well...

SPOT: I just want to say thank you for telling me and all my friends out in the audience about tattling.

SHAGGY: You are welcome. I'm glad I could help.

(The dogs exit waving to the audience.)

TATTLING

[1] Give some examples of tattling for safety, trouble or to be nice. Discuss what an adult's reaction to tattling can be to increase or decrease the amount of tattling.

[2] Some people tattle because they want attention, or they want to appear better than others. What are better ways of earning attention or praise? Why do you think some people avoid praise by doing things anonymously?

[3] Discuss why you wouldn't want to play with a tattletale. What are some ways they can encourage others to help them besides tattling?

[4] Talk about the story, "The Boy Who Cried Wolf," and other examples of how tattling causes problems for the tattletale and others.

[5] In a glass jar or other see-through container, put a button, marble, bean or other small object each time someone tattles. This will serve as a visual reminder not to tattle. Compare the number of items to the number the week before to reinforce the message, until tattling is no longer a problem.

LET'S BE FAIR AND SHARE
SHARING

CAST: Two Boys: Mike and Steven

PROPS: Toy cars, at least three—-Noise maker or squeaky toy

Approximately 5 Minutes

by Jill Hierstein-Morris

© 2024 Creatively Yours Publications

(Steven is on stage. There is a knock on the door and Steven turns to see who is there. He recognizes Mike and calls.)

STEVEN: Come in.

MIKE: Hi. Do you want to play?

STEVEN: Well...I...I'm not sure.

MIKE: What do you mean? Do you want to play or not?

STEVEN: Well, I would like to play with you if...If you will share.

MIKE: Share?

STEVEN: Yes. You always want to take over all the toys. That's no fun for me. Sometimes it makes me angry.

MIKE: Am I really as terrible as that?

STEVEN: Sometimes.

MIKE: Then I don't blame you for not wanting to play with me. I probably wouldn't want to play with me either. *(Mike turns and starts to leave.)*

STEVEN: Wait! I do like you. Please stay and play with me.

MIKE: What if I forget to share?

STEVEN: I have an idea. Wait here. I'll be right back. *(Exits).*

MIKE: *(To audience).* I wonder what he is up to.

(Steven enters holding a noisemaker and puts it down.)

MIKE: What's that for?

STEVEN: It's for time-outs.

MIKE: I don't understand.

STEVEN: In sports, when there is a disagreement, the players and coach stop to talk over what to do next, they call a time-out. If either of us is unhappy about the way the other is sharing, we can make a noise with the noisemaker. Then we can stop and talk about it. Okay?

MIKE: Okay.

STEVEN: But before we start to play, I need to put this car away. *(picks up a car).*

MIKE: (Uses the noisemaker). That's not fair. What if I want to play with that car?

STEVEN: I'm sorry. My grandmother gave it to me from a trip she took. If I put it away, NEITHER of us can play with it. I'm trying to be nice by not playing with it in front of you. Is that okay?

MIKE: I guess so. I have toys I wouldn't want anyone else to play with too.

STEVEN: *(He runs off with car then enters without it.)* You are a guest at my house, so which car do you want to play with first?

MIKE: *(Looks over cars, then points).* That one.

STEVEN: But that one is my favorite.

(Mike uses the noisemaker).

STEVEN: But you may play with it first.

MIKE: Okay. Thanks.

STEVEN: Are you sure you wouldn't rather play with one of these?

MIKE: No. Thank you.

(Steven uses the noisemaker.)

MIKE: What's wrong?

STEVEN: Nothing. I just want to suggest that we trade cars after a few minutes. There's a clock back there *(Points)*. You can play with the car for so many minutes, then I can play with it for so many minutes.

MIKE: Do we get the same number of minutes?

STEVEN: Yes. Let's say...Five minutes each.

MIKE: That sounds fair. *(They play for a few seconds, making car noises.)*

STEVEN: Time's up.

MIKE: Okay, let's trade. *(They trade toys and play for a few seconds.)*

STEVEN: Time to trade again. *(He extends the toy.)*

MIKE: (Uses *noisemaker*). I know it's my turn for this car, but I'm having fun with this one. Do we have to trade?

STEVEN: We can agree not to trade. I agree, do you?

MIKE: Yes.

STEVEN: So, it's okay. *(They play for a few more seconds.)* I'm getting hungry. I'll go ask mom if we can have a treat. *(Exits.)*

(Mike plays with his car, and Steven enters.)

STEVEN: Mom says there's a piece of cake. It's a big piece, so we can cut it in two.

MIKE: You'll make your half larger.

STEVEN: No, I won't.

MIKE: Yes, you will. I know you.

STEVEN: What makes you think I would?

MIKE: Because I would make my half larger if I cut it.

STEVEN: How about this, I'll cut the cake. You choose first. Or, if you prefer, you may cut it, and I will choose the first piece.

MIKE: Either way, it sounds like the pieces will be even, Steven. Hey! Even-Steven, that could be your nickname.

(They laugh and start to exit, then stop and look out at the audience.)

STEVEN: *(Looks at Mike).* Did you know there are a bunch of kids out there watching us?

MIKE: Sure. That's the audience.

STEVEN: Do you think they all share?

MIKE: They probably do. They look like a nice group of kids. Except for the one over there. *(He starts to point, and Steven pushes his arm down.)*

STEVEN: It's not polite to point.

MIKE: I'm sorry. Let's go eat.

(They exit together, waving at the audience.)

<u>**FOLLOW-UP EXERCISES**</u>

<u>**SHARING**</u>

[1] Kids are not the only ones who share. Discuss how your parents or other people share time, money and talents to make life more pleasant for you and others.

[2] Make a poster or public service announcement about sharing. Why should we share? Who should we share with? Why? What do we gain by sharing?

[3] Imagine a world in which no one shares. Would you want to live in this world? What things would be missing from your daily life?

[4] Discuss how the media (magazines, radio, television, and the internet) share information, opinions and ideas with the public. Why are they important to our happiness? What subtle messages about sharing are delivered by shows intended to entertain, such as situation comedies and cartoons?

[5] Share your talents in a telethon for a fictitious cause. Using your theme, tell why you are participating in the telethon, why you sympathize with the cause, and how their sharing will make things better for their recipients. Use logic, emotion, humor, and testimonials to appeal for help. Didn't it make you empathize with others and feel good about helping?

WHINY WILLIE
WHINING

CAST: Four Dogs—Mother, Willie, and two others

Approximately 6 Minutes

by Jill Hierstein-Morris

© 2024 Creatively Yours Publications

(Curtain opens with two dogs on one side of the stage. Willie enters from the opposite side, stops, looks around, but doesn't see the two dogs.)

DOG #1: Oh, no! Here comes Whiny Willie. He's no fun.

DOG #2: Yes. I don't like being around him. His whining drives me crazy.

DOG #1: Let's get out of here before he sees us. *(They run off stage.)*

(Willie walks to center stage then paces, mumbling to himself. Mother enters and Willie stops pacing when she reaches him.)

MOTHER: Hi, Willie. How was your day at the park? You didn't stay very long.

WILLIE: *(Whining).* It was awful. Nobody wants to play with me. What can I do all day?

MOTHER: You can run around the dog track.

WILLIE: I don't want to do that.

MOTHER: You could bury a bone or dig one up.

WILLIE: Naw. That's no fun.

MOTHER: You could chase the neighbor's fluffy cat.

WILLIE: She'd just scratch my nose. It still hurts from the last time.

MOTHER: Well, you could take a nap. You are a little grouchy.

WILLIE: Oh, come on, Mom.

MOTHER: If you don't like any of my suggestions, you'll have to think of something by yourself.

WILLIE: May I eat?

MOTHER: You may have a bone.

WILLIE: Naw.

MOTHER: There's still some dog chow in your bowl.

WILLIE: Yuk! Do we have any Dog Yummies?

MOTHER: Yes, but I'd rather you eat something that's good for you.

WILLIE: But I want Dog Yummies.

MOTHER: No.

WILLIE: But I want some. Please. Can't I just have one?

MOTHER: I said no.

WILLIE: The other puppies get Dog Yummies all the time.

MOTHER: The other puppies are not my concern. You are. Willie, do you realize how much of the day you spend whining?

WILLIE: Oh, Mom, I don't whine.

MOTHER: You certainly do. All the time. Why do you suppose you do it?

WILLIE: I don't know. I guess it's because things don't happen the way I want.

MOTHER: And you think you can change things by whining?

WILLIE: *(Shrugs).* Maybe, if I whine enough, you will change your mind.

MOTHER: But I don't change my mind, do I?

WILLIE: Not usually.

MOTHER: I end up getting angry with you. And you wind up in the doghouse.

WILLIE: But you never let me do what I want.

MOTHER: I do if I think it's good for you. You can't ALWAYS have things your way. It's not good for you and it's not fair to others. Maybe I would let you do more if you ask me nicely...And give me time to think about your requests. Whining just upsets me and makes me not want to let you do anything.

WILLIE: But I'm lonely, and SO bored.

MOTHER: That is because you whine. No one enjoys being around a whiner. I love you, Willie, but it's more difficult when you whine. I just want to get away from you or send you away from me, like to your room. I don't like your whining, and others don't either.

WILLIE: *(Willie clears his throat and proceeds without a whiney voice.)* How can I stop? I do it without even thinking about it.

MOTHER: I'll be glad to help you. I can remind you that you are whining, then you can stop, and maybe reword what you are saying. After a while, you will be able to break the habit.

WILLIE: Then will I be happier? And will I have friends to play with me?

MOTHER: It will take some time and practice, but it will be worth it. You will be happier, and able to do more things. Then the other pups will be more willing to play with you. Just watch out for the whining.

WILLIE: I will try really hard not to whine.

MOTHER: I will help you by ignoring you when you whine. I won't mean I don't love you when I ignore you. I do want you to learn that whining is a bad way of getting my attention.

WILLIE: Okay, Mom. May I go out to play?

MOTHER: Yes. Willie.

(Mother exits. Willie walks back and forth across the stage, and two pups enter.)

DOG #1: Oh, oh. There's Whiny Willie.

DOG #2: And he's spotted us.

WILLIE: *(Approaching the dogs)* Hi. May I play with you?

DOG #1: Well...

WILLIE: I'll be nice. I'll try not to whine. My mom told me why I need to stop whining, and I'm trying. You can remind me if I slip and start whining. Okay?

DOG #2: Is he for real?

DOG #1: We could give him a chance.

WILLIE: Oh, thank you. What do you two want to do?

DOG #2: We want to play ball, but we lost our ball in the shrubs.

WILLIE: I'd be glad to help you look for it. Or we could use mine.

DOG #2: Okay. Go get your ball. *(Willie runs off stage.)*

DOG #1: He isn't so bad when he doesn't whine. And he said we could remind him when he starts whining. It sounds like he is really trying to change.

DOG #2: Yea, he's not so bad. Let's help him get the ball.

DOG #1: *(The dogs start to leave together, then stop.)* I just thought of something. If he stops whining, we'll have to change his nickname.

DOG #2: You're right. We can't call him Whiny Willie if he doesn't whine.

DOG #1: We'll have to find out his REAL name.

DOG #2: You ask him.

DOG #1: No. I don't want to ask him. Why can't you ask him?

DOG#2: Oh, stop your whining.

(They laugh and exit.)

<u>**WHINING**</u>

[1] Write, discuss, or illustrate ways to break the habit of whining.

[2] Put together a campaign to "Stamp Out Whining." Make up a slogan, logo, or commercials. Present a program about whining for another classroom or group of children. Follow up with an open discussion of the problem.

[3] Discuss reasons for whining—to get attention, hurt feelings, frustration, selfishness, illness, hunger and exhaustion. What can be done about them?

[4] People who whine on television sometimes seem comical, but whining in real life is rarely funny. Discuss the differences. How do you feel when you are around a whiner? What do you think of them? How do you react?

[5] Why does ignoring the whiner help him stop? How could it make the situation worse? Do you think it is a good idea or not?

Book 2
STRESSES

STRANGERS—SAFETY TIPS

CAST: 3 Children: Buddy, Sue, Sid, 1-3 Strangers

PROPS: Cardboard car, Paper bag

Approximately 7 Minutes

by Jill Hierstein-Morris

© 2024 Creatively Yours Publications

BUDDY: *(Enters and stops center stage).* Hi, Kids! I've come to talk with you about strangers. Do you know what a stranger is? A stranger is any person you don't know. You don't know their name...You don't know where they live...And you've never seen them in your home.

Before you started school, the people in your class were strangers, and you were a stranger to them. When you got to know each other, you became friends. So, you see, all strangers aren't bad people. Has your mother or father ever told you not to talk to strangers? That's because it is VERY HARD to know if a stranger is a good person or a bad person. If you don't talk to any strangers, you won't have to worry about talking to the wrong kind.

Good and bad strangers look the same. Bad strangers don't look scary or ugly. Both kinds of strangers will be very friendly when they talk to you. But bad strangers may try to trick you into going somewhere with them. They could say they need your help to find a lost puppy, or that they found a bicycle and if you go with them, they will give the bike to you. They could even scare you into going with them by saying to come with them because something happened to your mom or dad. I know if anything happens to my parents, who they will send to get me. If someone else comes for me, they will know the secret word my parents and I decided to use to let me know they are a safe person.

(A stranger in a car enters and stops.)

STRANGER: Can you tell me where Elm Street is?

BUDDY: Three blocks that way. *(Points).*

STRANGER: I can't hear you.

BUDDY: *(Louder).* Three blocks that way. *(Points).*

STRANGER: I still can't hear you. Come closer to my car.

BUDDY: *(Aside).* Do I know his name? No. Do I know where he lives? No. Have I ever seen him in my home? No. I'd better run. *(He starts to run toward the front on the car, then stops.)* I should run in the other direction so I'm harder to follow. By the time he turns his car around, I'll be long gone. *(He runs toward the back of the car and off stage. The car exits in the opposite direction.)*

(Buddy enters, looking around.) I think I've lost him. *(Exits).*

SUE: *(Enters and walks slowly to the opposite side of the stage).*

STRANGER: *(Enters holding a paper bag marked "CANDY." He approaches the girl.)* Little girl, would you like some candy?

SUE: *(Aside).* I sure do love candy. But do I know his name? No. Do I know where he lives? No. Have I seen him in my home? No. *(Yells).* No, thank you! *(Sue runs off stage. Stranger exits in the other direction.)*

SID: *(Enters and crosses stage).*

STRANGER: *(Follows boy on stage and calls).* Sid!

SID: *(Turns to see the stranger, then says to audience).* He knows my name. Does that mean he's not a stranger? No. Bad strangers are very tricky. He could have heard someone call me by name or read it on my school bag. I don't know his name or address...*(Runs off stage).*

STRANGER: *(Exits).*

(Buddy, Sue and Sid enter talking together.)

SUE: I ran away from a stranger today. He offered me candy.

SID: Someone I don't know called me by my name. He was probably trying to trick me. I ran away.

BUDDY: A man asked me for directions to Elm Street. I told him where it was. But he pretended he couldn't hear and tried to get me to come closer to his car. I ran.

SUE: Strangers can be so sneaky. I ask myself the three key questions so I'll know if they're safe or scary. I can run fast too; I think I can keep myself safe, but I'm a little confused about telephone calls.

SID: What do you mean?

SUE: What if I'm at home and someone I don't know calls? I can't see them to ask myself the three questions, and running away from the phone seems silly.

BUDDY: Just ask who is calling and offer to take a message. Never tell them that you are alone. If they ask if your mom or dad is home, say they are busy and tell them to call back later.

SUE: I can do that. What do you do when someone on the computer wants to talk with you?

BUDDY: That's especially scary. Never agree to meet or privately chat with strangers on line. Don't give them information about where you live, where you go to school, details about your family, or other things that could lead them to you offline. If they are bad strangers; you don't want them to be able to find you. If you are playing a game with a chat function, you can mute the chat, so you don't have to worry about strangers talking to you.

SID: That sounds great, but what if I'm lost or need help? Can I ask a stranger to help me?

BUDDY: If you don't have your phone, you can ask a stranger to call the police for you. Just never go anywhere with a stranger. If they are good strangers, they won't mind bringing help for you.

SUE: Right. And if you call the police and they come to help in their police car, you need details. You must know your full name, your parent's full names, your street address, city, and your phone number including area code.

SID: It also helps to know where your parents work and what activities they may be participating in that day. Some places, like movies, or meetings at work, may make people turn off their phones. The more information you have, the sooner you will be home safe and sound.

BUDDY: Excellent advice. I know another really good way to be safe if a bad stranger is trying to bother me.

SUE: What's that?

BUDDY: I can scream...LOUDLY!

SID: I bet we can all do that. When I count to three, let's all scream. One...Two...Three *(Scream. If scream is weak, try again)*.

BUDDY: Wow! If all you kids can scream like that, and remember the other things we've talked about, we will all be safe.

SUE: Will you guys walk me home?

BUDDY: Sure. We are always safer in groups than when we are alone.

(They all exit, waving to the audience as they go.)

<u>STRANGERS</u>

[1] Make a poster about one of the ideas for dealing with bad strangers.

[2] Discuss some of the things strangers might tell kids to get them to go with them.

[3] Write, discuss or illustrate what you think a stranger looks like. We have images of handsome good guys and ugly bad guys. Discuss why these stereotypes are dangerous.

[4] Discuss the people in your community whose jobs are related to safety. What do they do? Do they wear uniforms or drive special vehicles? The discussion may be followed by a field trip to a police or fire station.

(5] Think of these and other strangers you meet. Would they be safe or unsafe to talk to? Why?

Your new teacher?

A man in the park?

People visiting your home?

A grocery store clerk?

A postal carrier?

A neighbor looking for his dog?

IT'S DARK IN HERE—FEAR OF THE DARK

CAST: Mother-—Jessica-her daughter

PROPS: Cot with bedding, toys, box

Approximately 5 Minutes

by Janet Tubbs

© 2024 Creatively Yours Publications

(Mother and Jessica enter bedroom.)

MOTHER: Time for bed, Jessica.

JESSICA: Oh, Mom, do I have to?

MOTHER: Yes, you do.

JESSICA: Someday, when I get older, I'll stay up all night if I want to.

MOTHER: I'm sure you will. But now it's time for bed.

JESSICA: Okay.

MOTHER: I'll help you put your toys away. *(They bend over and pick up toys and put them into a box.)* There. Ready?

JESSICA: Sure. I guess I'm kind of tired anyway.

MOTHER: Did you brush your teeth?

JESSICA: Yes. I brushed them right after dinner.

MOTHER: Good for you. Come on, hop into bed. Goodnight, honey, pleasant dreams.

JESSICA: Goodnight, Mom.

(Mother starts to leave. Lights are dimmed. Jessica lies down then pops up.)

JESSICA: Mom!

MOTHER: My goodness, what's the matter?

JESSICA: Oh, nothing, It's nothing. Goodnight.

MOTHER: Goodnight, honey. *(Mother starts to leave again.)*

JESSICA: Mom!

MOTHER: What is it, Jessica? *(Lights are turned back up.)*

JESSICA: Oh, well...It's nothing.

MOTHER: Come on. Tell me. And don't say it's nothing.

JESSICA: You'll laugh at me.

MOTHER: Laugh at you? No, I won't. I promise.

JESSICA: Okay. I think there's a monster in my closet.

MOTHER: A monster? Well, let's look and see. Come on, let's look together.

JESSICA: I don't think I want to.

MOTHER: It's safer if we look together.

JESSICA: Okay. *(Jessica rises and they look offstage into the closet.)*

MOTHER: See? Nothing but your clothes, shoes, and a little dust.

JESSICA: What's that? *(Pointing).*

MOTHER: What's what?

JESSICA: That thing...It's a ghost!

MOTHER: Do you mean your white bathrobe?

JESSICA: Is that what it is? What a relief. When you turned out the light, it looked like a ghost.

MOTHER: Oh, yes. I can see why it would look like a ghost. Except there are no such things as ghosts.

JESSICA: There isn't?

MOTHER: No, there isn't. You just thought your white robe was a ghost. It was your imagination playing tricks on you.

JESSICA: I guess so. Boy, do I feel better!

MOTHER: Are you ready to go to sleep now?

JESSICA: I think so…Except for one thing. Now you'll really think I'm being silly.

MOTHER: No, I won't. I promise. What is it?

JESSICA: Well, sometimes I think there are monsters under my bed.

MOTHER: Okay. Let's look.

JESSICA: Okay. Oh…Well maybe we shouldn't.

MOTHER: Why not? Don't you want to see if there is a monster under there?

JESSICA: No. I mean sure. I mean…

MOTHER: Jessica, is there something I should know?

JESSICA: You'll find out when you look under my bed. Remember today when you told me to clean my room?

MOTHER: Yes. Oh, no! You don't mean…?

JESSICA: Yup. Under my bed.

MOTHER: *(Bends down and looks).* Let's see. Oh, my goodness, Jessica! There's no room for a monster under here.

JESSICA: There isn't? Goodie! Maybe I should keep all my clothes and toys under my bed all the time.

MOTHER: Jessica...

JESSICA: Just kidding, mom. I'll clean it up tomorrow. But for now, could you leave the light on when you leave?

MOTHER: Yes. Jessica, it's good you told me you were afraid of the dark. There are lots of people who feel that way.

JESSICA: There are?

MOTHER: Sure. Even grownups are sometimes.

JESSICA: Are you?

MOTHER: Sometimes.

JESSICA: What do you do when you're afraid of the dark?

MOTHER: I leave a small night light on, just like I'm going to do for you. *(Goes to side of stage, light dims slightly).* It makes me feel better, so I can sleep. It will help you too.

JESSICA: Thanks, mom. And thanks for not laughing at me or getting mad. I love you.

MOTHER: I love you too, Jessica. Get your rest so you will have the energy to clean under your bed tomorrow. Goodnight. Sweet dreams.

(Jessica lies down and Mother exits.)

[1] Discuss things that make children fearful and share ways they have conquered their fears.

[2] Make ink blot pictures by putting paint or ink in the middle of a sheet of paper, folding it in half and applying pressure. When pictures are dry, have the children talk about what they see in the pictures and how, when we are afraid, simple things can become fearful things in our imaginations.

[3] Talk or write about what the monster under the bed is really like. He may be a lovable creature who is misunderstood because of his looks. Discuss how we judge people, and if they are fair assessments. What are common stereotypes?

[4] Discuss about special effects in movies and television. Explain that most of what happens is not real. Discuss how stage make-up, puppetry, special camera effects, miniaturization and other techniques are used to trick viewers into believing something is real when it isn't.

[5] Jessica's mother said it is safer to look into the closet together. Explain why it is usually safer to do things with someone else. Jessica saw a ghost, and her mother saw a bathrobe, then the two could decide who was correct. Ask for other examples of how our imaginations change what we see.

BRACES!

CAST: 3 Children—Dennis, Sarah, & Michele

Approximately 4 minutes

by C.R. Scheidies

© 2024 Creatively Yours Publications

(Dennis and Sarah enter.)

DENNIS: What's the matter Sarah? You haven't smiled all day. Are you getting teased about being "Beaver Mouth' again?

(Sarah shrugs).

DENNIS: Ah, come on, what's the matter?

(Sarah shakes her head no.)

MICHELE: *(Enters and joins them).* Leave her alone, Dennis. Can't you see she doesn't want to talk?

DENNIS: Well, why not? I've never seen her so quiet. Come on, Sarah.

SARAH: *(Angry).* All right, Dennis, if you must know, I have to get braces. Now just leave me alone.

DENNIS: You're going to get hardware?

SARAH: *(Frowning).* That's what I just said, didn't I?

DENNIS: *(Raises hands in defense).* All right. All right. I meant no harm. What's the problem anyway? Why are you so glum?

SARAH: How would you feel about wearing braces for a WHOLE year?

DENNIS: My older brother had to wear braces on his teeth for two years. It was a bit of a nuisance, but now he has great teeth. He's really glad that mom and dad made him go to the dentist.

SARAH: You're just saying that. I hate the idea of going to the dentist. Besides, everyone is going to laugh at me when they see my braces.

MICHELE: I'm not, and neither are your true friends. You can't help that you need braces. It's no different than getting a cast to help you heal a broken bone. I helps your body be better.

DENNIS: And who cares if some laugh. In a year you'll have great teeth. No one will be able to call you "Beaver Mouth" again.

MICHELE: Right, Sarah. Going to the dentist for braces might not be your idea of having good time but think of how great it will feel when it's all over and the braces come off. Then you'll think the dentist isn't so bad.

DENNIS: Your dentist cares about how you look, Sarah. He doesn't want to hurt you.

MICHELE: That reminds me of the first time my little brother had to go to the dentist. He was up all night screaming with a toothache. He screamed even more when he found out dad was taking him to the dentist.

SARAH: What happened? Was it scary?

MICHELE: He came home smiling. He said Doctor Carter was really nice. He even got a silly little toy for being good.

SARAH: But did it hurt?

MICHELE: He said it hurt a little, but the dentist numbed it and then it felt better. He heard the drill, but the dentist was very careful with it. The main thing is, he much preferred the treatment to a throbbing toothache.

DENNIS: See, It's no big deal, Sarah. I've been to the dentist lots of times. I've got three fillings...and I'm still alive. *(Teasing).* But then, we all know boys are braver than girls.

SARAH: No way, Dennis! I'll go. Maybe it won't be so bad. *(Teasingly).* It couldn't be if YOU survived it.

DENNIS: Oh, Sarah, you'll do just fine. When is your appointment?

SARAH: Tuesday at nine.

MICHELE: Terrific I have my check-up scheduled for ten. Do you want to go together?

SARAH: I'd like that.

DENNIS: I'll be with you in SPIRIT. *(Pretends to fly off stage, the girls laugh and exit.)*

FOLLOW-UP EXERCISES – BRACES

[1] Either visit a dental office or have a dentist come to speak to the class.

12] Discuss the different reasons for going to the dentist: Checkups, toothaches, braces and other procedures. Explain what steps the dentist might take in each case. (Be realistic about any pain or discomfort involved but emphasize the positive results.)

[3] Learn the parts of a tooth, the different types of teeth, and their purpose and placement in the mouth. Discuss how to keep teeth healthy through eating a balanced diet, restricting sweets and sticky foods, and with regular brushing.

[4] Have the students make a take-home chart on which they can keep track of the number or times they brush their teeth.

[5] Research the history of dentistry. Why would children prefer to go to a dentist today than a hundred years ago? What major advances have been made in technology, education, science and diet?

BABY BROTHER BLUES— NEW BABY

CAST: 2 Boys—Tim and Mike

Approximately 4 Minutes

by Jill Hierstein-Morris

© 2024 Creatively Yours Publications

(Tim enters.)

MIKE: *(Enters slowly with head down, lifts head slightly and looks at Tim).* Hi.

TIM: Hi. What's the matter, Mike? You look sad.

MIKE: I'm sad...And angry.

TIM: Why?

MIKE: Oh, it's my new baby brother. My mom and dad said having a brother was going to be great.

TIM: And it isn't?

MIKE: Not at all. He cries ALL the time!

TIM: Well, babies can't talk, so they have to cry when they need something. That's their only way of communicating.

MIKE: Oh, I know...But I don't understand why everyone thinks he's so great. They come to see him and say, "Oh, he's so cute." He's just a baby. And they give him toys. He isn't even old enough to play with toys.

TIM: It sounds to me like you're jealous.

MIKE: I am NOT! I just don't see what's so great about having a new baby in the house. He's boring. All he does is eat, sleep, get wet and drool. He can't talk and everyone makes goo-goo noises at him. Since he came home from the hospital, no one notices I'm around.

TIM: (Sympathetically). That sounds awful.

MIKE: It is. When I need something, I always have to wait until the baby is taken care of first. Then when I get upset, I get sent to my room to calm down.

TIM: You're lucky you are able to do things for yourself. And sometimes it's fun having a little brother. It will be better when he learns to walk and talk…except when he gets into your things.

MIKE: Oh, no. I hadn't even thought about that.

TIM: When he's older, you can do lots of things together.

MIKE: Like what?

TIM: Well, you could play board games with him. You can teach him how to play baseball and other sports. And when he gets older, he will look up to you and think you're the most important person in the world.

MIKE: But I don't feel very special now.

TIM: I'm sure when you were a baby, they treated you just like they are treating your brother now. And think of all the things that you can do that the baby can't.

MIKE: Like what?

TIM: You can talk, sing, dress yourself, eat pizza, go to the movies, have friends at school...You can do all kinds of things.

MIKE: But he gets all of mom's attention.

TIM: Maybe you could get more attention by helping your mom take care of your new brother. And tell her you would like to spend some time alone with her and your dad. They are probably so busy that they don't realize you are feeling left out.

MIKE: Okay. Do you think they still love me?

TIM: Of course, they do. I'm sure they love you at least as much as your baby brother. You are a family.

MIKE: A family...All four of us. Well, I think I'll go see if there is anything I can do to help my family. *(As exiting)*. See you later. And thanks.

TIM: You're welcome. Bye, Bye! (Waves and exits).

<u>**FOLLOW-UP EXERCISES – NEW BABY**</u>

[1] Discuss with the children what it is like to be an only child, the oldest, middle or youngest in the family. What is it like living in a large family, small family or blended family? What are the advantages and disadvantages of these different family styles?

[2] Let the children draw a family portrait and write a sentence or two about what makes each family member special.

[3] Do you think Mike's feelings of being left out are justified? What extra work is caused by a baby in the household? What things can older brothers or sisters do to help out?

[4] Getting a new brother or sister is one of life's major changes that affect the whole family. What are some other life changes? (Adoption, illness or death of a family member, separation or divorce, remarriage of the mother or father, blending families, a sibling starting school, going off to college, and many others.)

[5] Have the children ask their parents about their parents and grandparents. Then let them draw a family tree to show where they are in the family. Discuss how the tree will continue to grow as they get married and have children, and their children grow up and have families of their own.

A MOVING EXPERIENCE—MOVING

CAST: 2 Boys – Justin and Jerry

PROPS: Pencil and paper

Approximately 4 Minutes

by Jill Hierstein-Morris

© 2024 Creatively Yours Publications

(Jerry is on stage to one side. Justin rushes up to him.)

JUSTIN: Jerry, I have to talk to you!

JERRY: What's wrong, buddy?

JUSTIN: Mom and dad just told me we are going to move.

JERRY: Move? Where to?

JUSTIN: I don't know.

JERRY: Well, when are you going to move?

JUSTIN: I don't know.

JERRY: Will you still be going to school at (Insert school name)?

JUSTIN: I don't know.

JERRY: Are you staying in this city, state, or country?

JUSTIN: I don't know.

JERRY: Didn't they tell you anything about your move?

JUSTIN: Well...I guess I didn't give them a chance. When they said we would be moving, I ran outside. I felt like I had been kicked in the stomach. I just started playing baseball, and now we are going to move away. And I don't want to leave my friends.

JERRY: You could probably play baseball, no matter where you live. And if you don't know where you are moving, how do you know you will have to leave your friends?

JUSTIN: I guess I need more details.

JERRY: I think so. If you don't move very far, you might still go to the same school as all your friends. If you move but are still within driving distance, you can call or visit your friends to tell the about your exciting adventure.

JUSTIN: Adventure?

JERRY: Your move. All the exciting things you will discover in the new area where you move.

JUSTIN: But can I take all my toys? My dog? Will I like my new neighbors or school? There are so many things to worry about.

JERRY: *(While walking off stage)*. I'll be right back.

JUSTIN: Where are you going?

JERRY: You'll see in a minute. *(Exits and returns with a pencil and paper).* We are going to make a list of questions to ask your parents.

JUSTIN: Oh, that's a good idea.

JERRY: First, where are you moving to? If it's nearby, that will eliminate a lot of other questions. Second: Why are you moving? Maybe you just need a larger house, or maybe your dad's job makes a transfer necessary. Third: How far away, and will the climate be different? If it's far away, it would help to read about the area, and maybe visit your new school before the move.

JUSTIN: What about my dog and my toys?

JERRY: I'll add that to the list. You'll probably be able to take most of your stuff. If you can't take your dog, maybe you can help your family find her a good home.

JUSTIN: Will I make new friends fast?

JERRY: I don't think your mom and dad can promise that. But I don't think you will have to worry. Just be yourself and the new kids will like you just like us old friends do.

JUSTIN: Are there any other questions I should ask?

JERRY: There's one. Ask what you can do to help. Moving is hard work, and it goes much better if everyone pitches in. I'm sure your parents will appreciate anything you can do to assist.

JUSTIN: I sure am going to miss having you as a friend.

JERRY: I can still be your friend, no matter where you live. We can call and use the computer to keep up with each other's lives. We can still exchange school pictures. And we might even be able to visit each other sometimes. But before you cry and worry about leaving, we'd better find out where you are going.

JUSTIN: You're right. *(Takes the list).* I'm going home right now to get all the facts. Maybe all this worrying has been for nothing.

JERRY: I hope so.

JUSTIN: Me, too. But we'll be friends no matter what.

JERRY: No matter what, pal.

(They exit together)

<u>**FOLLOW-UP EXERCISES – MOVING**</u>

[1] Discuss things that may change and things that probably won't change when a family moves.

[2] Have the children pretend that they have to move. Let them select a place they would like to live. Have them draw a picture of the area and write a paragraph or two about what they think it would be like living there.

[3] When people move, they usually sort through their possessions and get rid of unnecessary things. Have the students think about things that might be discarded and environmentally safe ways of discarding those items. Recycling outgrown clothes and household goods by giving them to charitable organizations, giving old toys or arts and craft supplies to local preschools or kindergartens, selling useful items through a garage sale, of if your town provides taking recyclable materials to collection bins, all are excellent ways to dispose of unwanted items.

[4] Sometimes moving means starting at a new school. Have the children suggest ways to meet and become friends with the kids at their new school or in their new neighborhood.

[5] Ask the class to share their experiences with moving, and if possible, add stories of your own. Read a book or show a movie about moving. If possible, invite someone from a foreign country to speak to the class about the cultural differences they encountered when they moved to this country.

JUST LIKE YOU— HANDICAPS

CAST: Jan—-Kim (limps)—-David (blind)

PROPS: Dark glasses & cane (dowel painted white) for David

Approximately 4 Minutes

by C. R. Scheidies

© 2024 Creatively Yours Publications

(Kim and Jan are talking quietly as they walk slowly across the stage. David slowly approaches the girls.)

JAN: Look at that boy. How does he do it? How does he know where he is going?

KIM: He feels his way with a cane. He gets familiar with places he goes to often.

JAN: Oh, do you know him Kim? What's it like knowing someone like that?

KIM: Like what, Jan? He's a human being just like you and me.

JAN: *(Embarrassed).* Well, you know...he's handicapped. He's different from the rest of us.

KIM: Is that what you think of me since my accident, Jan? Am I less of a person because my leg doesn't work right anymore?

JAN: Of course not. You're my best friend, as you always were. Your leg doesn't change that!

KIM: It's the same with David, or any other disabled person. We are just people with feelings like you. We have good days and bad days, are happy or sad. We aren't different on the inside.

DAVID: Kim, is that you?

KIM: Yes, David. I am here with my friend Jan. *(To Jan).* I met David when I was in the hospital. He came to visit me after my accident,

JAN: *(Hesitantly).* Hello, David. Nice to see you. I didn't mean...SEE...I meant...*(Embarrassed).*

DAVID: *(Chuckling).* It's all right, Jan. You don't need to change how you talk because I can't see. It's only an expression.

KIM: Are you getting acquainted with the neighborhood, David? I'm surprised to see you out and about without George. *(To Jan).* That's his seeing-eye dog.

DAVID: He's down with a cold. Thankfully, it's nothing worse. He'll be fine in a day or two. In the meantime, I had to go back to using my cane. It's been awhile, and truthfully, Kim, I think I've lost my way. I was glad to hear your voice. Maybe you could steer me back home.

KIM: I'll be glad to walk with you. I haven't seen you for such a long time. Jan, do you want walk with us as I show David the way?

JAN: I...um...Do you want me to take your arm or something, David? *(Uncomfortable).* To tell you the truth, I don't know what to say or what to do around...you know, disabled people.

DAVID: Oh, so you act differently around Kim than your other friends?

JAN: No, but...

DAVID: Although our handicaps may not be the same, we aren't different. Just treat us like you would anyone without a handicap.

JAN: But what if you need help?

KIM: It is sometimes hard for disabled people to ask for help. So, if you want to know what you can do for someone, just ask. Remember when I first came home from the hospital, and you volunteered to help me? I helped you with your math handicap, and you helped me as I learned how to use my leg again.

JAN: I think I understand. You're saying we all have our problems. Some problems, like yours and David's, are just easier to see.

DAVID: Now you're getting it, Jan. It really doesn't matter how big or how small we are, or how disabled we are. We are all people. Our lives have value and meaning.

KIM: We should care about one another, no matter what. And we should treat each other with respect.

JAN: Message received. Each of us are special in our own way. I have an idea, Kim. Why don't we make a slight detour and show David how to get to the ice cream shop?

DAVID: Lead on friends.

(All laugh and exit.)

[1] Provide blindfolds, crutches, a wheelchair, and other items. for the class. Have them pretend they are disabled. What can they do? What can't they do? How difficult is it for them to go through doorways, climb stairs, use bathrooms, or pick up and carry things?

[2] Invite an individual with disabilities to come and speak to the class about their abilities and their disability.

[3] Discuss the worth of each student. Is a person worth less because of a handicap? What can students do to help someone who is physically or mentally disabled? How would they wish to be treated if suddenly found themselves handicapped by an accident or illness?

[4] Have the students paint or draw a picture holding a brush or pen between their teeth. As they share their creations, explain that some good artists who cannot use their hands or arms, actually paint this way. Have them talk about the difficulty they had with their pictures. When disabled people, just like people without handicaps, keep trying, they often succeed.

[5] Give the students the following list of individuals to read up on. Explain that each of these persons was considered handicapped. Answer the questions: Why was this person famous? What was his/her handicap? How did the handicap limit the person? Did the handicap in any way help the person become famous? Can you think of others to add to the list?

    Ludwig van Beethoven

    Sarah Bernhardt

    Louis Braille

    Thomas A. Edison

    Elizabeth Barret Browning

    Ben Hogan

    Hellen A. Keller

    John Milton

    Franklin D. Roosevelt

    Stevie Wonder

    Marlee Matlin

Book 3
TOUCHY TOPICS

NOT EVERYONE DOES
SELF RESPECT

CAST: 4 boys: Tom, Dick, Harry and Paul

Approximate Time: 6.5 Minutes

By Jill Hierstein-Morris

© 2024 Creatively Yours Publications

(Tom, Dick and Harry are on stage in a group. Paul enters and approaches them.)

TOM: Hey, guys, there's the birdwatcher.

DICK: Tweet. Tweet. Tweet.

HARRY: How are your fine, feathered friends today?

TOM: If it weren't for his fine, feathered friends, he wouldn't have any friends at all...Except for the eggheads.

DICK: Why don't you forget about all the bird stuff?

PAUL: I enjoy birdwatching. It doesn't hurt anyone.

TOM: Everyone thinks you are crazy.

PAUL: What I think of myself is more important than what others think of me.

(Paul exits. The other boys exit after a short pause. Paul comes back on stage followed by Tom.)

TOM: Paul, did you study for the math test we're having today?

PAUL: Yes.

TOM: You are a brainy guy, how about letting me copy off of your test paper?

PAUL: No.

TOM: Why not? I was out with the guys last night. I didn't have time to study. A nice guy like you wouldn't want me to fail the test, would you?

PAUL: I wouldn't want you to cheat either. I worked hard to memorize all the stuff for the test. You should have too. I won't help you to cheat.

TOM: It's not cheating. I just want to borrow your answers. I will learn them later. I just need your help today.

PAUL: If you were really concerned about learning the material, you would have studied.

TOM: Oh, you're just trying to be a goody-goody.

PAUL: I'm just trying to do what I feel is right. And trying to help you do what is right too.

TOM: Gee thanks. Who needs you? *(Exits).*

PAUL: *(Facing audience).* I just can't do things I don't believe are right. *(Exits).*

(Tom, Dick, and Harry enter and stand talking.)

DICK: I just purchased some fine stuff for tonight. I have smokes and a variety of pills. We are going to fly high tonight. Come over about eight o'clock. My parents will be out of the house by then. No one will bother us.

TOM: Sounds great.

HARRY: Yea, great.

(Paul enters to one side of the stage.)

TOM: There's Paul...Let's invite him.

HARRY: Are you kidding? He wouldn't do anything like that.

TOM: I know, I just want to see how he will react. Ask him, Dick.

DICK: *(Approaching Paul, followed by the others).* Hi, Paul. Do you want to come over to Dick's place tonight and do some drugs?

PAUL: No way!

DICK: Oh, come on. Grow up.

PAUL: No. It doesn't show you're grown up to do drugs. It shows you're weak. Drugs are dangerous!

TOM: They won't hurt you. Parents just say they will hurt you because they don't want you to have any fun.

PAUL: They can hurt you, and I don't want anything to do with them.

DICK: You're just interested in birds. You should like birdwatching because you are a Big Chicken!

PAUL: I'm not a chicken.

TOM: Then join us.

PAUL: No.

DICK: Everyone does it.

PAUL: I don't have to do something I believe is wrong, just because everyone else does it.

TOM: You're right, Dick. He's a chicken.

DICK: Bock, Bock, Chicken.

(The three boys make chicken sounds as Paul exits. Then they exit. After a short pause, Paul comes back on stage. Harry enters and walks up to Paul.)

HARRY: Hi, Paul. I am sorry about teasing you. I had to or the guys would have given me a bad time.

PAUL: That's okay.

HARRY: Paul, can I ask you a question?

PAUL: Sure.

HARRY: How do you have the courage to stand up for what you believe in?

PAUL: What do you mean?

HARRY: Well...I don't like always going along with the crowd. And I don't like fooling around with drugs. But I'm afraid not to. I really admire the way you resist those guys. I think you are very brave. I wish I could be.

PAUL: You can be.

HARRY: No. I can't. I'm scared.

PAUL: Scared of what?

HARRY: That I won't have any friends.

PAUL: Sure, you will. They may not be the friends you have now, but you'll have friends...The kind you can feel comfortable with. Ones that won't pressure you into doing things you don't want to do.

HARRY: I'd be afraid to stand up to the guys. They will tease me, like they do you.

PAUL: I know it won't be easy. You will be lonely sometimes. You might wonder if it's all worth it, but if you really want to, you can break away and start over with new friends.

HARRY: Do you mean, the only way is to ride out the storm and start all over again?

PAUL: I'm afraid so.

HARRY: I just don't know if I can do it.

PAUL: I'll help if I can. And there are programs to help you deal with the drugs.

HARRY: I don't know if I can be without friends until I can make new friends.

PAUL: Friends will come and go, but you always have to live with yourself.

HARRY: That's true.

PAUL: I will be here whenever you want to talk.

HARRY: You'd really do that for me?

PAUL: Sure. I think everyone should be free to be themselves.

HARRY: Gee, you really are a GREAT guy.

PAUL: No. Just a guy...Doing what I believe in and hoping others can too.

HARRY: I like that. Can I buy you an ice cream cone?

PAUL: Sounds good to me.

(They exit).

<u>**FOLLOW-UP EXERCISES**</u>

<u>**SELF RESPECT**</u>

[1] Discuss how pressure is exerted by teasing and name-calling. Is there a Paul in your class or group? Are you like Paul? Do you want to be? What does being true to yourself mean to you?

[2] Consider these cliches: A bird in the hand is worth two in the bush. Sticks and stones may break my bones, but names will never hurt me. There's safety in numbers. Include others you can think of. Are these true or false in relation to peer pressure?

[3] What are some of the problems Harry will have making new friends and breaking away from his old friends? Will it be worth it? Why or why not?

[4] Pressure groups (organizations, political parties, lobbyists and others) use a variety of methods to sell people of their beliefs. When are these pressure groups important? When are they dangerous?

[5] Talk about techniques used to persuade—logic, emotional appeals, ridicule, threats, promises, and violence. Divide into two groups, one favoring red socks, the other favoring green socks. Stage a debate between the two groups. Write or discuss which arguments you were swayed by and why. How does the ability to communicate by the speakers influence your views?

SAYING NO

CAST: Three Girls: Karen, Cathy, Elisha – Boy: Roy

PROP: Pack of cigarettes

Approximately 6 Minutes

By Donna M. Hammontree

© 2024 Creatively Yours Publications

(Karen and Cathy enter from opposite sides of the stage.)

KAREN: Hi, Cathy. Do you want to go walking in the park?

CATHY: Sure, Karen.

ROY: *(Entering).* Where are you going, Cathy?

CATHY: Karen and I are going to the park.

ROY: Cathy, I need to ask a favor. Dad told me to mow the lawn. Can you do it for me? Please?

CATHY: I don't know, Roy.

ROY: Sure, you can, sis. You and Karen can play any time.

CATHY: Well, I don't know...Roy...I...

ROY: I knew I could depend on you. See you later. I'm going swimming.

CATHY: But...

ROY: *(Exiting).* Thanks.

CATHY: Sorry, Karen. It looks like I have to go home and cut the grass for Roy.

KAREN: You should have told him no.

CATHY: That's not so easy to do.

ELISHA: *(Entering).* Hey Cathy, I've been looking for you.

CATHY: Why?

ELISHA: Well, I just bought a pack of cigarettes, and now I have to go home.

CATHY: You bought what?

ELISHA: You know, cigarettes.

CATHY: What's that got to do with me?

ELISHA: I can't take cigarettes home with me. My mom might find them. Do you know how long she'd ground me for if she knew I was smoking? Forever! So, you'll take them for me, won't you?

CATHY: Elisha...I...

ELISHA: *(Hands pack to Cathy)*. Great! And don't forget to bring them to me at school tomorrow.

CATHY: But...

ELISHA: *(Exiting)*. See you two later. Thanks.

KAREN: Whew! You have a real problem.

CATHY: Boy, do I. Look at these cigarettes. I don't even smoke. What if MY mom finds them?

KAREN: Yes. Those cigarettes are a problem too; but I was talking about how you can't seem to say no to anyone.

CATHY: What are you talking about? I can say no.

KAREN: Did you want to cut the grass for Roy?

CATHY: No.

KAREN: Did you want to hold Elisha's cigarettes for her?

CATHY: Definitely not!

KAREN: Then why didn't you just tell them both no?

CATHY: I just couldn't. Mom says to always be nice to other people.

KAREN: Does you mom expect you to mow the lawn for Roy?

CATHY: No. I weed the flower garden for my chore.

KAREN: Would your mom want you to carry around or hide Elisha's cigarettes?

CATHY: No way.

KAREN: So, your mother wouldn't care if you told SOME people no. She wouldn't consider it rude or anything?

CATHY: No....She wouldn't.

KAREN: Sometimes I can't tell people no because I want them to like me.

CATHY: Really?

KAREN: I'm afraid if I say no, they will get mad and no longer want to be my friend.

CATHY: That's why I didn't say no to Elisha.

KAREN: The only thing is, if they expect you to do things you don't want to do, maybe they weren't such great friends to begin with. She was just using you. Can we try something? Let's practice saying, NO.

CATHY: *(Giggling).* That's silly, Karen.

KAREN: What's so silly about it? If you could have told Roy and Elisha no, we could go to the park. I'll ask you some questions, and you tell me no. *(Thinking).* Will you do my English report for me?

CATHY: You're a better student than I am. *(Weakly).* No.

KAREN: *(Laughing).* That was pretty soft, Cathy. I can tell you'd do my report if I asked you again. And don't stop to rationalize your answer. If you don't want to do something, just say no. This time say it more loudly. Can I borrow ten dollars?

CATHY: Well...I...*(Weakly).* No.

KAREN: *(Turns to kids in the audience).* Hey, you kids out there, Cathy needs some help saying no. When I ask a question, please say no with Cathy. Ready? Will you skip school with me tomorrow?

CATHY: *(With audience).* No!

KAREN: I bet you can do better than that. Will you help me steal all the money in the teacher's purse?

CATHY: *(With audience).* No!

KAREN: That was great. Let's drink some of my dad's beer.

CATHY: *(With audience).* No!

KAREN: Do you want to buy some drugs?

CATHY: *(With audience).* No!

KAREN: You are all pretty good at that. Now, Cathy, you need to practice by yourself again. Will you babysit for me tonight?

CATHY: *(Strongly).* No, I won't.

KAREN: Perfect. Now you've got it.

CATHY: The audience out there was so good at saying no to the things they didn't want to do. They were a lot of help.

ROY: *(Entering)*. Cathy, why are you still here? You are still going to cut the grass for me, aren't you?

CATHY: *(Firm, but not mean)*. No, Roy. Sorry, I won't be cutting the grass for you. I have other plans.

ROY: Oh...Okay. I guess I'd better get home and get busy, then. *(Exits)*.

ELISHA: *(Enters)*. Do you still have my cigarettes, Cathy?

CATHY: *(Handing them to Elisha)*. Here they are. I won't be holding them for you anymore. They could get me in trouble. And I don't even smoke.

ELISHA: Okay. I had better get rid of them. I don't want to get caught with them, and I should stop smoking them anyway. *(Exits)*.

KAREN: Way to go, Cathy! I'm proud of you.

CATHY: It worked. I said no nicely, and they didn't even get mad.

KAREN: So, can we go to the park now?

CATHY: NO. *(Laughs)*. Just practicing. Let's go.

(The two girls exit together.)

<u>**FOLLOW-UP EXERCISES**</u>

<u>**SAYING NO**</u>

[1] Why is saying no so difficult? What were Cathy's reasons for doing favors for others when she really didn't want to? Were they valid or not? What kind of trouble can trying to please everyone cause?

[2] "Just Say No," is one slogan for dealing with pressure from peers. Have the children come up with their own slogans, then make posters to display on the walls.

[3] In the play, Karen says, "If they expect you to do things you don't want to do, maybe they weren't such great friends to begin with." Do you agree or disagree with this statement? What should friends expect, and not expect from you?

[4] Does it take more character to give in to others or stand up for what you believe is the best for you? If you do everything friends ask you to do, can it be dangerous for you?

[5] Why did Karen insist that Cathy practice saying no? Is there a parallel between practicing saying no and practicing a baseball pitch or tennis serve. Do they build confidence? Are they easier with practice?

<u>**CHILD ABUSE**</u>

(FOR THE TEACHER)

Children must always be alerted to the danger of strangers: talking with, accepting gifts from, and going with people they don't know. However, the majority of child abusers are people they know, and often a member of the family. Children are often sexually abused from an early age, and having no basis for comparison, may feel it is expected of them and acceptable. The abuser often frightens children by saying:

If you tell, I will go to jail.

If you tell your mom or dad, they will be mad at you.

If you tell, I'll hurt you, your family, or your pet.

Children may intuitively know that continued intimate contact is wrong but are confused because the perpetrator is a loving member of the family. They must be told that any action that causes discomfort, physically or emotionally, is wrong and someone must be told in order to stop the abuse.

Adults often find it difficult to broach such a sensitive topic with a child. They may prefer not to know or are reluctant to admit their suspicions. These methods of ignoring the problem are dangerous and unhealthy. Sexual abuse occurs in every strata of society and is more pervasive than commonly thought.

Too much emphasis on the subject and repeated questioning may create an atmosphere of fear. Not enough emphasis offers little or no protection for the innocent child.

Hopefully, the following simple script will serve as an icebreaker between parent and child, resulting in improved, free-flowing dialogue. Puppetry offers non-threatening and enjoyable play that frequently results in revealing deep-seated concerns and emotions such as fear, guilt, anger, and more.

DON'T TOUCH ME!
CHILD ABUSE

CAST: Mother, Child

Approximately 3 Minutes

By Janet Tubbs

(Mother enters followed by Child.)

MOTHER: Come on, honey, it's time to go to Uncle Joe's. I have to go to work.

CHILD: I don't want to.

MOTHER: You don't want to? Why?

CHILD: I just don't. I don't like him.

MOTHER: But he's your uncle.

CHILD: I don't care. I don't like him.

MOTHER: Uncle Joe loves you. Doesn't he fix you good meals when you're there?

CHILD: Yes.

MOTHER: And doesn't he play games with you?

CHILD: That's just it, mom! I don't like the kind of games he wants to play.

MOTHER: What do you mean? What kind of games?

CHILD: Oh, they're all different, but they all end up the same.

MOTHER: What do you mean?

CHILD: Well, he likes to wrestle on the floor a lot. And when he gets me down, he kisses me and touches me. He says it's all part of the game. But sometimes he hurts me.

MOTHER: Why didn't you tell me this before?

CHILD: Uncle Joe said it was only a game. If I told you about it, he'd go to jail and you would be very mad at me.

MOTHER: When did he start playing these games with you?

CHILD: A long time ago. When you went to work and he started watching me.

MOTHER: That's been almost a year! And you never said anything to me.

CHILD: I wanted to, but I was afraid you would be mad at me. I was afraid maybe you would think I was making it up. Or even that you'd call the police and he'd go to jail.

MOTHER: That's exactly what I'm going to do, honey. People who hurt little boys and girls are doing something wrong, and we have to call the police when we know people are doing something wrong.

CHILD: Even if it's your own uncle?

MOTHER: Yes, even if it's your own uncle, or father, or aunt or anybody.

CHILD: I'm sure glad I told you. I couldn't figure out why I didn't like it when Uncle Joe kissed me. I mean, it was different from when you or daddy kiss me. I didn't like it. I didn't want him to touch me.

MOTHER: I'm glad you told me. Any time anybody hurts you, or even makes you feel uncomfortable being with them, you should tell somebody. It could be grandma, a police officer, a neighbor, or some other person you trust. As long as you don't say anything, they'll keep on playing those kinds of games with you and other children. No one has the right to hurt you...No one. Do you understand what I mean?

CHILD: I sure do, mom, and I know what I'd say to somebody like him from now on.

MOTHER: What?

CHILD: I'd say DON'T TOUCH ME!

MOTHER: You're a good kid. Let me call work, then we will head for the police station.

(They exit.)

<u>**FOLLOW-UP EXERCISES**</u>

<u>**CHILD ABUSE**</u>

[1] Discuss things an abuser might say or do to keep a child from telling an adult what they are doing with the child.

[2] What are the differences between good touches (hugs or pats that make the child feel wanted and loved) and bad touches (those that make a child feel uncomfortable or hurt the child.)

[3] Talk about trust. When is it necessary not to trust what an adult might say?

[4] Invite a child abuse counselor or school nurse to visit the classroom. Have her explain that in a situation of abuse, the child is not bad or wrong, but the victim of an adult. Let her explain that there is help available to people who do these kinds of things, but most abusers don't get help until they are confronted. By telling of abusive situations, you protect yourself and make it possible for the abuser to get the help they need to stop the abusive behavior.

[5] Read a book about a safety-related topic and stress that telling an adult when someone makes you feel uncomfortable is as important to their safety as telling when someone is playing with matches.

TOO MANY BRUISES
PHYSICAL ABUSE

CAST: Three girls: Shawna, Darlene and Kim

Approximate Time 7 Minutes

By Donna M. Hammontree

© 2024 Creatively Yours Publications

(Darlene and Kim are talking on stage as Shawna enters.)

DARLENE: Hi, Shawna.

SHAWNA: Hi, Darlene. Hi, Kim. What's going on?

DARLENE: We just got back from shopping with my mom. Boy, does she look at everything in the mall!

KIM: No kidding. She had us going into clothing stores, furniture stores, book stores, even sporting goods stores. I'm totally exhausted!

DARLENE: Yes, but it was fun.

KIM: Yes. *(Pause)*. Shawna, what did you do to your arm? It's all bruised, and it has some spots that look like burns.

DARLENE: OH! It hurts me just to look at it.

SHAWNA: *(Sputtering)*. I...Uh...Was...Uh...Just cooking some...hamburgers, I mean chicken, and the grease splattered on my arm and burned me.

DARLENE: You know how to cook chicken?

SHAWNA: I'm just learning.

KIM: I help mom in the kitchen, but I think I'll stick to setting the table. Cooking chicken looks painful.

DARLENE: You sure get hurt a lot, Shawna. *(Faces Kim)*. Don't you think so Kim?

KIM: Yes. It was just a couple of weeks ago that you ran into a door and got a bad bruise on your face.

SHAWNA: I'm just clumsy. That's all.

DARLENE: And I remember that time last summer when we went swimming. You had red marks on your back. You said you fell down some stairs.

KIM: You must really be accident prone, Shawna.

DARLENE: Hey, Shawna, you know, those burns on your arm look a little like a picture I saw in my mom's health magazine last week.

SHAWNA: Really?

DARLENE: Yes. The article was about child abuse. The child's parent had burned the child with a cigarette. The burns were small and round, just like yours.

SHAWNA: (Defensively) You must be dumb or something, Darlene. What do you know? I got these burns frying pork chops.

KIM: I thought you said you got the burns cooking chicken.

SHAWNA: Pork chops, chicken, same thing.

DARLENE: Yes. Pigs and chickens look just alike. Especially when they open their snouts and say "Cluck, Cluck." *(Darlene and Kim laugh.)*

SHAWNA: I got mixed up. That's all.

KIM: I read that article on child abuse too. It said that kids who get beaten up by their parents think they deserve it.

SHAWNA: If the kids DON'T deserve it, why do the parents hurt their kids?

KIM: Parents who abuse their kids are usually angry at themselves. They get all frustrated and take it out on their children. The kids feel like they are no good, and they deserve to be abused or locked in closets.

DARLENE: Locked in closets? That sounds horrible. I guess my little swats to the seat aren't so bad after all.

KIM: Some kids get locked in a closet for days with nothing to eat. There's a difference between being taught right from wrong and being mistreated.

DARLENE: That's awful. I bet abused kids feel really sad and lonely inside.

SHAWNA: Yeah.

KIM: Some parents abuse their children by neglecting them. The kids are left home alone for a week or so. Or they aren't given food to eat. Some parents don't bathe their children or make sure they go to school.

DARLENE: And some parents make their children feel really bad inside. They call their kids names like stupid or worthless.

KIM: That's abuse too. The children start believing they are stupid when they really aren't.

SHAWNA: They're not?

KIM: No, Shawna. They are good kids.

DARLENE: The article said the abused kids don't tell on their parents because they love them, even though their moms or dads hurt them. The kids will even lie about their sores and injuries to protect their parents. Abused kids are afraid they will have to live in a foster home, or that their parents will be sent to jail, if they tell.

SHAWNA: What does happen to a kid if she tells on her parents?

KIM: Some kids are sent to foster homes until their parents get help to handle their emotions better. Some go to live with grandparents or aunts.

DARLENE: My grandparents would spoil me rotten. That might be fun.

KIM: Some abused children stay at home with one parent, and the parent who hurts the kids has to move out. Parents who mistreat their kids can get help.

SHAWNA: What kind of help?

KIM: There are special doctors trained to help adults deal with their anger and learn how to stop hurting their children.

SHAWNA: Does the parent still have to go to jail, Kim?

KIM: Not if a judge thinks the parent can change.

SHAWNA: Where can a kid who's being abused get help? I mean, don't think my dad beats me or anything...I'm just curious.

DARLENE: I would tell my teacher, doctor or a police officer.

KIM: Or you, I mean the kid, could tell an adult person at church, or a trusted neighbor.

SHAWNA: What if no one helps and your parents get so mad they hurt you worse than before?

KIM: If a child tells an adult that he or she is being abused by their parents, the adult HAS to call social services and get help for the child. It's the law.

SHAWNA: Oh.

DARLENE: It would be hard to tell on a parent, but I think they should. Otherwise, things could get worse and worse.

KIM: Everyone deserves a safe place to live. It's not the child's fault this parent has a problem.

DARLENE: The way I see it, the child who tells would be helping their whole family. They would be protecting theirs brothers and sisters from abuse. And they would help their parents get help in dealing with their problems.

SHAWNA: *(To herself)*. So, the child would help everyone by telling on her parents. *(To Darlene and Kim)*. I'll see you two later. I've got things to do. *(Exiting)*. Maybe I'll go talk to the school nurse tomorrow.

KIM: Darlene, she's thinking about what we said.

DARLENE: I think she's tired of being hurt. Nobody should be abused.

KIM: I'm glad we talked to her.

DARLENE: Me too. I'm really glad she listened.

KIM: Come on, Darlene. Helping others makes me hungry. I'm going to get an apple.

DARLENE: Kim, EVERYTHING makes you hungry. But I think our good deed makes us deserving of a piece of my mom's chocolate cake.

KIM: What are we waiting for?

(They exit together.)

<u>**FOLLOW-UP EXERCISES**</u>

<u>**PHYSICAL ABUSE**</u>

[1] Why did Shawna try to hide the fact that she was being abused? Why did her friends feel it was important to talk to her about it? How did they recognize the signs of abuse?

[2] Invite a professional to talk to the class about types of abuse and ways the children can get it stopped.

[3] Sometimes the distinction between discipline and abuse is not clear in the child's mind. Discuss what discipline is and why it is used. Explain what abuse is and why it is so important to break the chain of abuse from generation to generation.

[4] Make "feeling masks" to show how things that happen make us feel inside. Use the masks as a way of expressing and discussing feelings about abuse and other problems.

[5] Think up slogans about abuse, neglect and anger. Use these on posters or booklets. Discuss the ways people deal with anger. Which are positive and which are negative? Why?

STOP HITTING MOM
ESCAPING ABUSE

CAST: Three children—Melissa, Barry, Lisa

Mother—-Voice only

Approximately 7 minutes

By Donna M. Hammontree

© 2024 Creatively Yours Publications

(Barry and Lisa are on stage. Melissa enters.)

MELISSA: Hi. Why are you two whispering? And what are you so nervous about? A person would think you were planning an escape.

BARRY: Shhh, Melissa, not so loud.

MELISSA: *(Quieter and with more concern).* What's going on?

LISA: We are going to escape.

BARRY: *(To Lisa).* Lisa, we're not supposed to tell.

MELISSA: You've got to tell me now. Please! You have made me so curious.

BARRY: Oh, all right. I guess we can tell you if you promise not to tell anyone else.

MELISSA: I promise.

BARRY: Lisa, Mom and I are running away from here.

MELISSA: Why? I don't want you to leave. I like playing with you and Lisa.

LISA: And I like riding bikes with you. But we have to go.

MELISSA: But why? I don't understand.

LISA: It's because my dad...hits my mom

MELISSA: *(Still confused).* Your dad hits your mom?

LISA: Yes...Um...maybe more than hits. He gives her bruises, black eyes and sometimes kicks her.

MELISSA: *(Turning to Barry).* What's Lisa talking about, Barry?

BARRY: She's telling you what we've had to live with for as long as I can remember. Dad drinks a lot of beer. Then he gets mad at mom and starts beating her up.

MELISSA: Do you have to watch him hit her?

BARRY: Sometimes we see it all. But if he beats her late at night, we lie in bed and hear them.

LISA: It makes me cry.

MELISSA: I can't imagine. My parents hardly ever yell at each other. What does your mother do that's so bad? She must do terrible things to deserve being beaten.

LISA: One night she cooked chicken for supper, and dad wanted ham.

BARRY: Another time dad didn't like the way she set the dinner table. But no matter what, no one deserves to be beaten.

MELISSA: Sounds like really small things to get upset about.

BARRY: He got so upset he knocked all the food and dishes off the table and onto the floor. Then he stood over her yelling while he made her clean it up.

LISA: I wanted to help mom. I don't like to see her cry. But dad sent me to my room.

BARRY: One night I tried to get dad to fight with me instead of my mom.

MELISSA: Did he hurt you?

BARRY: No. It just made him madder and he hit mom harder. Mom told me to go to my room.

MELISSA: I bet you hate your dad. He has always been so nice to me.

LISA: I love my dad. He is nice most of the time. His drinking is the problem.

BARRY: I love dad too. I just don't like the way he hurts mom.

MELISSA: Why does she let him hit her?

BARRY: She tries to get away, but he's stronger than she is.

MELISSA: Why hasn't she left him before now?

LISA: We all left him one time before.

BARRY: But we came back because dad begged us to. He does love all of us, even mom. She loves him too. And he said he would change.

MELISSA: I guess it can be really hard to change. I can't even stop biting my finger nails.

BARRY: Plus, mom couldn't get a good enough job to pay for a place to live, our food and clothes.

MELISSA: When you leave today where will you go? Will you be homeless?

LISA: We are going to a shelter.

MELISSA: What's a shelter?

BARRY: It's a big house where women who are abused and their children can go to live. Most of the women have been mistreated by their husbands, fathers, stepfathers or even the mom's boyfriend. They get counseling and training to help the women find jobs.

MELISSA: It sounds like an awful place.

LISA: It's a nice place. It has toys, beds and food.

BARRY: And it's a safe place. No one knows where it is except for the people who need to go there to hide.

MELISSA: Will you still go to school?

BARRY: We will but not at the same school. They are always afraid dads might try to kidnap their kids.

MELISSA: Oh.

BARRY: The workers at the shelter are good to us. They will talk with mom about her problems. And teach her skills to get a job so she can support us.

LISA: Barry, do you remember Cathy?

BARRY: Yes. She was the children's counselor.

LISA: She played games with us.

BARRY: Cathy also talked with us about our feelings. She really cared about how we felt toward mom and dad.

MELISSA: Why?

BARRY: Because she said it's really hard for kids to watch their parents fight. She said some boys grow up to beat their moms and later their wives. Boys learn to be just like their fathers. They learn by example.

LISA: And girls whose parents fight have to be careful too. They might grow up and marry a man who behaves just like their dad.

MELISSA: Are there lots of kids who live with parents who fight?

BARRY: Yes. There are hundreds of thousands of homes in our country that have violence in them.

LISA: Last night our parents had a big fight. Barry called the police.

BARRY: I had to do something. Mom was really hurt.

LISA: The police put dad in jail.

BARRY: And we have to leave before he gets home today. I bet he's really mad now.

MELISSA: I'm really sorry.

BARRY: The policeman said dad can get help. There's a special group in town that helps fathers quit hurting their wives.

MELISSA: That's good. I hope he gets better.

LISA: I do too. I sure am going to miss him.

BARRY: I am too. But we have to go. Everyone deserves a safe place to live.

MOM: *(Calling from off-stage).* Barry! Lisa! We're all packed. Let's go.

BARRY: Bye, Melissa. Don't worry. Hopefully, dad will get help and we'll be home soon.

MELISSA: I'm glad you'll be home soon, and that it will be safer when you come home.

(Melissa waves as Barry and Lisa exit.)

MELISSA: I'll miss you. Bye you two. *(Exits).*

<u>**ESCAPING ABUSE**</u>

[1] Discuss the agencies in your community that help families in crisis.

[2] Talk about feelings. How are the children in the skit touched by feelings of love, loyalty, fear and other emotions? Explain the meaning of empathy. Have the class talk about how they would feel in the roles of Barry, Lisa and Melissa.

[3] Have the children draw pictures of what they think a shelter looks like. Invite a social worker to come to class and tell about shelters and the services they provide.

[4] Compile a list of people children might be able to turn to in a crisis situation.

[5] Discuss how humans, especially children, learn from example. What are some of the things you have learned from the example your parents have shown you? What things do you do that set a good or bad example for your younger brothers and sisters?

DEATH AND TELEVISION

CAST: Ashley, a girl -—Aaron, her brother

PROPS: Television (decorated box) – recorded television western.

Approximately 4 Minutes

By Jill Hierstein-Morris

© 2024 Creatively Yours Publications

(Aaron is watching television. Ashley enters.)

ASHLEY: Hi. What are you watching?

AARON: Just some detective show. This guy is about to shoot it out with the bad guy. *(Making shooting motions)*. Get him! Pow! Pow! Kill him!

ASHLEY: *(Shocked)*. Aaron, that's awful!

AARON: *(Confused)*. What's awful?

ASHLEY: Yelling for someone to KILL someone.

AARON: Oh, sis, don't get upset…It's just television. People die all the time on TV. It's no big deal. That guy will be alive on another show next week.

ASHLEY: It just upsets me that you enjoy the violent, impersonal death they show on TV. Mom says most people don't die at all like they show on television. Most die from old age…Their bodies just wear out.

AARON: People die from accidents...or diseases, earthquakes, floods and stuff. I see it on the evening news.

ASHLEY: Yes, but far more die after a long life. And people have lots of feelings when someone dies. Feelings that they hardly ever show on television. There's loneliness because they won't be seeing that person again. You remember all the good things that you and they did when you were together. Sometimes people feel sad or guilty because they weren't more kind to the dead person. And they didn't get to tell them how much they loved them before they died.

AARON: I felt that way when Rover died. I thought because I didn't always feed him or keep his water dish full, I might have caused his death.

ASHLEY: But Rover was hit by a car.

AARON: I know. But he might have been hit because he was running across the street to find something to eat. I felt bad too because I didn't get to say goodbye. Remember, mom and dad said it would upset me to see him after the car hit him?

ASHLEY: And because we didn't see him dead, it was hard to believe he really was dead. I kept thinking it was a big mistake and he would come back alive in a day or two.

AARON: Really? Me, too.

ASHLEY: When I finally accepted the fact that Rover was dead, I got very angry with Rover for being so careless. And I was mad at the driver of the car for hitting him.

AARON: Me, too. I hated being around my friends who had dogs...I guess I was jealous because they had dogs to love. I didn't.

ASHLEY: Yes. We probably would have felt much worse if he had been hit, lived, but was badly hurt. It would have been hard to see him suffering day after day.

AARON: It's too bad that dogs can't be injured or die then pop back to normal, like they do in cartoons.

ASHLEY: Death isn't at all like on television.

AARON: I know. Death is more like a deep cut.

ASHLEY: A what?

AARON: A deep cut. When someone dies, whether it's a pet or a person you love, it hurts a whole lot at first. Gradually, the cut heals, but it leaves a scar...all the memories of good times you had with them when they were alive.

ASHLEY: So true. Are you ever afraid of dying?

AARON: Sure. Everyone is a little afraid of the unknown. But everyone will die someday. That's nature's way of making room for all the new babies that are born.

ASHLEY: I guess so. But just remember, death is not something to cheer about on TV. It's serious and involves a lot of feelings. So what else is on the television?

AARON: Dust.

ASHLEY: Get serious.

AARON: There's a fairy tale. *(Sarcastically)*. We could watch someone come back to life with a kiss or magic spell.

ASHLEY: Never mind. I'm going outside to ride my bike. *(She exits.)*

(Aaron changes channels on television. Sounds come from a western—Draw, Mister! Bang, Bang! Or similar. Aaron goes up and turns off the TV).

AARON: For some reason, television just isn't as exciting as it used to be.

(Exits).

DEATH AND TELEVISION

[1] Have the children share their experiences with death. Talk about feelings and fears concerning death. You can also discuss life after death and the idea of being reunited with our loved ones who passed away, when we die.

[2] Discuss how television deals with emotions. Why are most deaths on TV violent? What other topics have the children noticed that are inaccurately portrayed?

[3] In what ways do cartoons and fairy tales distort a child's conception of death?

[4] Talk about life cycles of people and animals, and the stages of development between life and death. You may want to tie this in with a science lesson.

[5] Invite a funeral director to speak to older children about how our society prepares the dead for burial. You may also want to discuss how other cultures differ in the way they prepare their dead for burial or burial procedures.

Don't miss out!

Visit the website below and you can sign up to receive emails whenever Jill Hierstein-Morris publishes a new book. There's no charge and no obligation.

https://books2read.com/r/B-A-FRTMC-KXNIF

BOOKS 2 READ

Connecting independent readers to independent writers.